READY TO LAUNCH

Jesus-centered parenting in
a child-centered world

J.D. & VERONICA GREEAR

curriculum developed by
David and Jen Thompson;
Will and Julie Toburen;
and Spence Shelton

LifeWay Press®
Nashville, Tennessee

Published by LifeWay Press®. © 2014 J.D. and Veronica Greear
Reprinted 2015

ISBN: 978-1-4300-3205-2 · Item: 005644088
Dewey decimal classification: 649
Subject headings: PARENTING \ CHILD REARING \ CHURCH WORK WITH CHILDREN

Scripture quotations are from The Holy Bible, English Standard Version® (ESV®),
copyright © 2001 by Crossway, a publishing ministry of Good News Publishers.
Used by permission. All rights reserved.

To order additional copies of this resource, order online at *www.lifeway.com*; write LifeWay Small
Groups: One LifeWay Plaza, Nashville, TN 37234-0152; fax order to 615.251.5933; or call toll-free
1.800.458.2772.

Printed in the United States of America.

Adult Ministry Publishing; LifeWay Church Resources; One LifeWay Plaza; Nashville, TN 37234-0152

CONTENTS

ABOUT THE AUTHORS

J.D. and Veronica Greear: J.D. is Lead Pastor at The Summit Church in Raleigh-Durham, N.C. He is also the author of *Gospel: Recovering the Power that Made Christianity Revolutionary* (2011) and *Stop Asking Jesus into Your Heart: How to Know for Sure You are Saved* (2013). J.D. and his beautiful, relatable, fun, and passionate wife, Veronica, live in Raleigh, NC and are raising four ridiculously cute kids: Kharis, Alethia, Ryah, and Adon. J.D. completed his Ph.D. in Theology at Southeastern Baptist Theological Seminary where he is also a faculty member, and Veronica is a graduate of the University of Virginia.

David and Jen Thompson: David is Lead Pastor for Executive Leadership at The Summit Church in Raleigh-Durham, NC. He and his wife, Jen, both graduated from Wake Forest University. David completed his Masters of Divinity at Southeastern Seminary in Wake Forest, NC and just recently finished his Doctorate of Ministry at Southern Baptist Theological Seminary in Kentucky. They have four children, Caroline, Ellie, James, and Cole.

Will and Julie Toburen: Will is Executive Pastor of Discipleship Ministries at The Summit Church in Raleigh-Durham, NC. He and his wife, Julie, both graduated from North Carolina State University. Will completed his Masters in Divinity at Southeastern Seminary in Wake Forest, NC. They have four children, Abby, Jackson, Blake, and Alex.

Spence Shelton is Small-Groups Pastor at The Summit Church in Raleigh-Durham, NC. His first book, *The People of God*, co-authored with Trevor Joy, released in May 2014. Spence and his wife, Courtney, are the proud parents of Zeke, Ben, Ellie, and Haddie.

J.D. & Veronica with Kharis, Alethia, Ryah, and Adon

➤ LETTER FROM J.D.

As a parent of four children, I'm grateful for every bit of parenting advice the Bible gives. Perhaps most valuable is the vision for parenting God gives us through the pen of Solomon in Psalm 127:4-5: "Like arrows in the hand of a warrior are the children of one's youth. Blessed is the man who fills his quiver with them!"

For years I missed the importance of the imagery here. Solomon compares the children of Israel to a fist full of arrows. And what's the purpose of an arrow? To be shot out in the battle!

See, before we can ask, "How should I raise these children?" we have to ask, "Why did God give me these kids?" If the purpose is to send them out into God's battle—ultimately, to let them go—then that must undergird all we do in parenting.

Many of us, we fear, take the legitimate desire for our kids' safety and magnify it into a dominating idol. Sure, we are responsible for our kids' safety and must take that responsibility very seriously. But the ultimate point of an arrow is to fly on a mission. As Reggie Joiner writes in *Parenting Beyond Your Capacity*, "We're fine if our children never climb a mountain as long as it guarantees they never get hurt. But what if your children were made for the mountains? … The ultimate mission of the family is not to protect your children from all harm but to mobilize them for the mission of God. … It is possible to hold on to our kids so tightly that we forget the ultimate goal of parenting is to let go."[1]

Furthermore, when we take children God created to be arrows and instead treat them like a piece of furniture that we plan to accentuate our lives—we not only stunt their development, we also keep them from knowing God at all! God made our kids to be adventurous. And there's nothing more adventurous than loving and serving God. Our desire to saturate them in comfort and luxury actually does them the greatest harm.

So are you looking to keep your "arrows" safely in the quiver—unharmed, but ultimately useless? Or will you trustingly launch them out? Veronica and I are excited about this study for parents and how God will work in your lives as result of the truths revealed in Scripture about preparing our children for God's mission. We're glad you're along for the journey. Now let's get … *Ready to Launch*.

1. Reggie Joiner, *Parenting Beyond Your Capacity* (Colorado Springs: David C. Cook, 2010), 180.

HOW TO USE THIS STUDY

Welcome to this seven-session experience in intentional parenting! We hope your group experience results in a greater understanding of God's design for parents, as well as a deeper understanding of how the church community plays an important role in raising children.

To best make use of this study, let your first session together be an introduction. Plan to watch the introduction video and spend time getting to know one another. Make sure each group member receives a copy of the Bible study book so that they come prepared for the first group discussion.

The first page of each session should give you an introduction or a brief glimpse of the topic you'll be discussing as a group. Read this section in preparation for your group time.

Each session will contain the following format:

START: These are questions your group leader may use to begin conversation before the *Watch* and *Discuss* sections. Some of these questions will ask you to reflect back on your activity from a previous session, which can also be a time for you to get ideas from other group members and encourage one another. Other questions may be used as an icebreaker to get discussion started.

WATCH: J.D. and Veronica Greear will lead a teaching time on the topic for each session. Watching the video together and taking notes will enrich your discussion and may provide additional insight into the session's discussion questions.

DISCUSS: This time is designed to build on the lessons taught in the video by looking at a separate passage of Scripture. This works best when you work through the questions individually before gathering together. Come into the discussion ready to share what God showed you in your own study. If you're stumped on a question, you can look forward to asking for insight from group members during your time together.

WRAP-UP: As you end your group time, key points are given that should have been highlighted in your time together. Use these points to reemphasize the overarching message of each session.

PRAY: One way to describe prayer is to believe God on behalf of another person. As a group, spend time praying for one another as you begin this journey toward parenting God's way. Use the points to help guide you.

FAMILY ACTION PLAN: For each session, we've provided a practical step to help you put into action what you've learned from God's Word about parenting. Take time in the first few days after your study to work on this assignment. You'll often need more than one sitting to complete it. Feel free to come back to certain sessions if you need to rework or reevaluate your answers. You will likely need to schedule time to discuss these Scriptures, concepts and ideas with your spouse or family members. There is a chart on pages 110-111 for guidance while you're participating in the study and for your reference afterwards.

PERSONAL REFLECTION: Two devotions are included for each session. Take time to read and interact with these as you meet with God for the first days following your group time. The topics will address concepts you've just studied with your group, encouraging you to read additional Scripture passages and answer some reflection questions.

Let's get started!

LOVE IS NOT ENOUGH

PSALM 78:1-8

PROVERBS 2:1-10

"Desperate times call for desperate measures."

Whoever coined that phrase must have been a parent. If they weren't, surely they had a window into our home during one of those harrowing moments usually striking between the time school lets out and the time heads hit the pillow. If we're honest, much of our parenting is a reaction to the messes and mistakes our children are making all around us. We never wanted to be reactionary parents, yet it feels like that's all we have the energy to do. The great news is that God designed parenting to be a better, more fulfilling job than you may be experiencing right now.

God intends to send our children out like arrows. Psalm 127:4 describes it like "arrows in the hand of a warrior are the children of one's youth." We (David and Jen) recently gave our 7-year-old a Nerf® bow and arrow set. His first shot was hasty and clumsy, falling short of his intended target, which just so happened to be me. Thankfully the stakes are low with a foam-tip arrow in the front yard.

As the day went on, he took his time with each shot, lining up his arrow more carefully and choosing wisely where to shoot. In order to hit his target, he had to step back and prepare. Once he planted his feet, chose his target, and took aim, he hit doors, windows, and siblings with accuracy. Once he learned to prepare his shot, he became much more accurate.

This study is your preparation. By stepping back from the urgent call of spilled cereal, math tests, broken curfews or college applications, you can begin to seek the mind of God on how and where to shoot the arrows God has entrusted to you.

➤ START

Name people you would call good parents. What makes you choose those people?

What areas of parenting do you hope this study addresses?

➤ WATCH

GOAL: To clarify the purpose of our role as parents.

VIDEO HIGHLIGHTS:

1. Love is simply not enough when it comes to raising children.

2. Parenting comes with a weighty responsibility attached to it.

3. Scripture instructs fathers to be the spiritual leaders; discipline doesn't just fall on mothers' shoulders.

Watch Session 1: *Love is Not Enough.*
Use the notes page to record key quotes and ideas that stand out to you.

NOTES

_____

_____

_____

_____

_____

_____

_____

_____

_____

_____

_____

_____

_____

_____

_____

_____

_____

_____

_____

_____

_____

_____

_____

_____

Video sessions available for purchase at **www.lifeway.com/readytolaunch**

➤ DISCUSS

The first books of the Old Testament recount Israel's miraculous plight from captivity in Egypt to freedom in the promised land of Canaan. That journey from slavery to freedom is a picture of a greater spiritual reality. Just like Israel, we too were once slaves. Instead of being slaves to another nation, however, we were slaves to sin. Just as God delivered Israel, He also delivered us. The price of our deliverance from sin was death. He broke the shackles of sin by paying for our freedom in His own blood. To set us free, He paid our ransom by sacrificing His Son's life. Jesus died in our place as a payment for our sin, securing our freedom. Now Jesus has gone to prepare for us a greater promised land in heaven where He is our reward.

Psalm 78 was written to remind Israel, and us, to passionately tell the story of God's deliverance and faithfulness to generation after generation. God designed this to happen primarily through the family, with fathers and mothers taking every opportunity to teach their children the mighty works of God.

Give ear, O my people, to my teaching;

incline your ears to the words of my mouth!

I will open my mouth in a parable;

I will utter dark sayings from of old,

things we have heard and known,

that our fathers have told us.

We will not hide them from their children,

but tell to the coming generation

the glorious deeds of the LORD, and his might,

and the wonders that he has done.

PSALM 78:1-4

What does the psalmist have to say about the role of parents in this passage?

What steps are you currently taking to "tell to the coming generation the glorious deeds of the LORD, and his might, and the wonders that he has done"?

Recognizing our lives are crowded, what competes for your attention in a way that keeps you from faithfully executing your role as a parent?

He established a testimony in Jacob

and appointed a law in Israel,

which he commanded our fathers

to teach to their children,

that the next generation might know them,

the children yet unborn,

and arise and tell them to their children,

so that they should set their hope in God

and not forget the works of God,

but keep his commandments;

and that they should not be like their fathers,

a stubborn and rebellious generation,

a generation whose heart was not steadfast,

whose spirit was not faithful to God.

PSALM 78:5-8

With this passage as your guide, what are the benefits of faithfully teaching your children about God's greatness and power to save?

If applicable, describe a time within your own family that you have seen this type of faith heritage, where the glorious truth of God was taught and children set their hope in Him.

Raising a generation that will "set their hope in God" (Ps. 78:7) requires much more than just a commitment to love our children. We need tremendous wisdom to know how to shape their affections, draw boundaries, encourage and listen, discipline appropriately, and so much more. Proverbs 2 reminds us where to find wisdom as well as wisdom's many benefits.

My son, if you receive my words

and treasure up my commandments with you,

making your ear attentive to wisdom

and inclining your heart to understanding;

yes, if you call out for insight

and raise your voice for understanding,

if you seek it like silver

and search for it as for hidden treasures,

then you will understand the fear of the LORD

and find the knowledge of God.

For the LORD gives wisdom;

from his mouth come knowledge and understanding;

he stores up sound wisdom for the upright;

he is a shield to those who walk in integrity,

guarding the paths of justice

and watching over the way of his saints.

Then you will understand righteousness and justice

and equity, every good path;

for wisdom will come into your heart,

and knowledge will be pleasant to your soul.

PROVERBS 2:1-10

What specific circumstances are you currently facing with your children where you are in desperate need of wisdom?

Solomon assures us that the Lord will graciously supply all the wisdom we need to live, which of course includes wisdom in parenting. However, we must passionately seek after wisdom as we would search after something of tremendous worth.

When it comes to parenting, in what ways are you actively pursuing or needing to begin pursuing wisdom?

➤ WRAP-UP

1. Parents bear the primary responsibility for the discipleship of their children.

2. The goal for parents is to lead their children to set their hope in God and proclaim the gospel to the next generation.

3. Parenting requires more than love; it takes wisdom.

4. Wisdom must be pursued with great tenacity.

➤ PRAY

Spend the next few minutes praying with and for one another. Use the points below for guidance.

- Thank God for promising to give you everything you need to faithfully fulfill your role as a parent.

- Pray that each of your children will set their hope in God and delight in Him above all else.

- Ask God to give you wisdom to navigate all the challenges and pressures of parenting.

Family Action Plan

THE FAMILY MISSION STATEMENT

Part of stepping back and preparing to launch can be creating a family mission statement. Stephen Covey describes a family mission statement as "a combined, unified expression from all family members of what your family is all about—what it is you really want to do and be—and the principles you choose to govern your family life."[1] So, a family mission statement can be a tool to help your children remember and reflect on the core values and goals you've established as a family.

Here are five practical steps to help develop a family mission statement:

STEP #1: ENGAGE THE WHOLE FAMILY.
This is a great exercise for the entire family. Set aside a specific time to cast a vision with your children for why a family mission statement is important. The more your children feel part of the process the more likely they'll embrace it. Here are a few questions to begin the process:

- What do we want to characterize our family for generations to come?
- How would we want others to describe our family?
- How can we best use our talents and gifts to share Jesus with others?

STEP #2: IDENTIFY SPECIFIC GOALS AND VALUES BASED ON SCRIPTURE.
As you talk with your children about God's purpose for their lives, take time to discuss specific values and goals you have for the family. Also let your children speak into the process by sharing specific things God is putting on their hearts.

STEP #3: WORK TOGETHER TO CRAFT A STATEMENT.
Here's where you can get really creative. There's no one format that your family mission statement needs to take. It may take the form of a "motto," an acrostic using your family's last name, or some other creative form. No one size fits all. With young children, you'll be doing the work. With older children or teenagers, this is a great opportunity to let their voices be heard.

STEP #4: CREATIVELY DISPLAY AND REINFORCE YOUR FAMILY MISSION STATEMENT.
In order to keep the family mission statement in front of your family, look
for ways to prominently display it in your home. Also try and celebrate when
a family member honors a value or accomplishes a goal you've identified.
Reinforcement is the key to your mission statement taking root.

STEP #5: EVALUATE PERIODICALLY.
You may find as your children grow and mature that you need to modify your
mission statement. Evaluating periodically will allow you to adjust for the
different seasons of life your family will go through. If intentional parenting is
new to any of you, be encouraged that this will always be a work in progress.

**Use the space below to jot down some ideas. Then start to formulate an
initial draft of your Family Mission Statement.**

PERSONAL REFLECTION

Do Not Labor in Vain

> *Unless the LORD builds the house, those who*
> *build it labor in vain.*
>
> **PSALM 127:1**

For many mothers, the word *labor* quickly conjures up memories of childbirth. It does for me (Jen). I remember the first moments of labor contractions with our first child, hoping they were real—but fearing they might be false labor. My husband was ready to drive to the hospital after watching me dramatically curl up on the floor, while I claimed this wasn't the real thing. He had given up medical school for a religion degree and had no intentions of delivering a baby. I, however, definitely did not want to drive to the hospital with my bags packed, get our family all excited, and then return home. I was determined not to misdiagnose labor. My pride was on the line.

I wanted it to be the real labor that would give us our sweet daughter, Caroline. And thankfully, it was. I feel the same way at times about parenting. I don't want my labor to be in vain, and I definitely don't want to be embarrassed by my mistakes. I'd love to see immediate results as my kids bound in the door after school each afternoon, talking about how God worked through their math test, declaring their deep love for being with our family, and jumping right in to share the load of household chores.

But since we're not there yet, I know Psalm 127 must be true. Our family desperately needs the Lord to build our family and our home. We have a house and a literal roof over our heads, but we need so much more.

We need to create an environment where our children don't admire our righteousness and excellent parenting techniques, but instead adore our Savior. We need a house where our children can be assured grace is present and bountifully handed out, even if it's alongside consequences. We need to believe the gospel so deeply that we tell it over and over again to our children.

What makes it hard for you to give grace to your children?

Even if one particular afternoon routine was gloriously grace-filled, you can be sure the next day is going to bring chaos or strife. It's the nature of how much we need Jesus.

On a good day, what are you tempted to take credit for that God really deserves?

What is one way you believe God wants to build your house through this study?

➤ PERSONAL REFLECTION

Prioritize Your Vertical Relationship

> *Blessed is everyone who fears the L*ORD*, who walks in his*
> *ways! You shall eat the fruit of the labor of your hands; you*
> *shall be blessed, and it shall be well with you. Your wife will*
> *be like a fruitful vine within your house; your children will*
> *be like olive shoots around your table. Behold, thus shall the*
> *man be blessed who fears the L*ORD*.*
>
> **PSALM 128:1-4**

Charles Spurgeon, a well-known pastor in England in the 19th century, wrote, "The fear of God is the corner-stone of all blessedness. We must reverence the ever-blessed God before we can be blessed ourselves."[2] His point is simple: our willingness to delight in Christ above all else is the beginning point to gaining wisdom for every area of our lives—including parenting. In other words, our vertical connection to God leads to horizontal effectiveness in parenting.

As parents (Will and Julie) we long to see our children use their gifts and abilities to glorify God and engage in His mission for the church. We recognize, however, that their preparation begins with our lives being fully surrendered to Christ. The author of Hebrews exhorts us:

> *Let us also lay aside every weight, and sin which clings so*
> *closely, and let us run with endurance the race that is set*
> *before us, looking to Jesus, the founder and perfecter of our*
> *faith, who for the joy that was set before him endured the*
> *cross, despising the shame, and is seated at the right hand of*
> *the throne of God.*
>
> **HEBREWS 12:1-2**

The challenge is clear: we need to constantly look to Jesus and prioritize our walk with Him above all else. But we all know at times that's easier said than done. Our lives can become chaotic and we often find ourselves living under the tyranny of the urgent. Lunches need to be made, homework assignments completed, schedules kept—and that's just the kids! Often the first thing that falls to the wayside when our lives become busy is the space to spend time with God. When our vertical relationship isn't prioritized, we feel the consequences all around—including with our kids.

What could you do to improve the quality of time you spend with God?

What is the single biggest time-waster in your life and what can you do to change this?

What one step could you take to improve your prayer life?

1. Stephen R. Covey, *The 7 Habits of Highly Effective Families* (New York: Golden Books, 1997), 72.
2. Charles Spurgeon, *The Treasury of David* (New York: Funk & Wagnalls, 1886), 43.

OUR PRIMARY RESPONSIBILITY

Deuteronomy 6:4-9

Ephesians 5:22-25

Matthew 5:23-24

David and I (Jen) love military movies. Even though I often hide my eyes through a major portion of the film, I want to see the victory. I can remember several scenes where one soldier walks out of the battle, covered with scars and tears, holding his head up proudly because the enemy was defeated. In that victorious scene it's easy to forget all of the little moments that made that glorious moment possible.

Parenting is a battle. Can I get an *Amen* from someone? And like in wartime, these battles are won in the little moments. The phrase *gaining ground* was coined on the battlefield, referring to how an army would steadily advance, little by little, across the field of battle. Gaining ground was usually slow and hard, and required great focus on the objective while in the line of fire. In one battle you could move backward and forward dozens of times, making perseverance and courage invaluable assets to an army.

As we attempt to love our kids with the mind of God, we are in a battle. We have a goal of loving our children as God does and one day sending them out into the world to share that same love with others. To get there, we need a strategy for gaining ground. We need to know how to battle in the trenches of daily parenting in a way that pushes us toward our goal.

Deuteronomy 6 is God's strategy for how we gain ground in our parenting. The battle is fought with constant reminders of Jesus' perfect love for our children. It is fought with "I'm sorry" and "Will you forgive me?" and "Can we try that again?" and "What do you think God's Word has to say about that?"

And it will be fought minute-by-minute and hour-by-hour. Let's get started.

➤ START

What is your favorite war or military movie? What is it that you like about that movie? *Saving Private Ryan*

Have you ever thought your family was reenacting a war movie? How so?

Describe the last situation where you heard "I'm sorry" at your house.

➤ WATCH

GOAL: To communicate that our primary responsibility is to teach our children the gospel.

VIDEO HIGHLIGHTS:

1. The primary responsibility of both the church and the home is to teach the next generation the gospel.

2. Our children are the inheritance that we leave behind to teach other generations the gospel.

3. Bad news: there are no perfect children or parents. Good news: the Bible tells beautiful stories of redemption within the dysfunction of families—families probably much more messed up than yours!

Watch Session 2: *Our Primary Responsibility.*
Use the notes page to record key quotes and ideas that stand out to you.

NOTES

- Teach Gospel
- Ask for forgiveness at Home
- God took Families with Dsyfunction and gave Redemption

Are you teaching the Gospel?

Is Jesus a priority? or is it More important in getting your Children in College?

* Your actions speak so clearly. not what you say.

Model the Gospel.

➤ DISCUSS

In the last session we were reminded that the goal of parenting, in partnership with the church, is to lead the next generation to set their hope in God. To gain ground we must drive the gospel deep into their hearts. In Deuteronomy 6 God reminds Israel, and subsequently us, to take advantage of every opportunity to drive the gospel deep into the hearts of the next generation.

> *Hear, O Israel: The LORD our God, the LORD is one. You shall love the LORD your God with all your heart and with all your soul and with all your might. And these words that I command you today shall be on your heart. You shall teach them diligently to your children, and shall talk of them when you sit in your house, and when you walk by the way, and when you lie down, and when you rise. You shall bind them as a sign on your hand, and they shall be as frontlets between your eyes. You shall write them on the doorposts of your house and on your gates.*
>
> **DEUTERONOMY 6:4-9**

Verse 6 uses the word *diligently* to describe how we should teach and apply the Word of God to the next generation. How are you currently building times for teaching your children into the regular rhythms of your week?

Where in the weekly rhythms of family life could you build in times of teaching and applying God's Word?

Jesus also taught this very important principle in Mark 4 where He used a parable to get His point across. Jesus told the story of a sower who scattered seed on various types of soil. When the seed was thrown on the hard, rocky, or thorny soil the seed was never able to take root and bring forth a harvest. The problem in each case was that the seed never went deep enough. But Jesus also described a good soil, that when seed was sown, took root and brought forth a bountiful harvest. The picture is clear: when the gospel is planted deep into the heart the result is a life that glorifies God and advances His kingdom.

What barriers do you face that keep you from deeply planting the gospel in the hearts of your children?

What practical steps can you take to begin alleviating these barriers?

Planting these gospel seeds and teaching your children about Jesus is most effectively done by their observations of you as parents. This is called modeling the gospel. There are many ways we can model the gospel for the next generation. How we respond to suffering and injustice, how we handle our finances, and how we care for the oppressed are just a few. Two other beautiful pictures of the gospel are found in how we seek and extend forgiveness to others.

> *So if you are offering your gift at the altar and there remember that your brother has something against you, leave your gift there before the altar and go. First be reconciled to your brother, and then come and offer your gift.*
> **MATTHEW 5:23-24**

Based on Jesus' teaching, how should we respond when we've wronged another person? Why is this so difficult?

Think of a time when you wronged your children and had to seek their forgiveness. How could seeking their forgiveness encourage them to pursue the gospel?

Wives, submit to your own husbands, as to the Lord. For the husband is the head of the wife even as Christ is the head of the church, his body, and is himself its Savior. Now as the church submits to Christ, so also wives should submit in everything to their husbands. Husbands, love your wives, as Christ loved the church and gave himself up for her.

EPHESIANS 5:22-25

Paul challenges wives to "submit to their husbands" in everything. What does submission teach children about their relationship with Christ?

How does a husband loving his wife "as Christ loved the church" (v. 25) impact the next generation?

➤ WRAP-UP

1. In order for the next generation to set their hope in God they must drive the gospel deep.

2. Driving the gospel deep requires that we teach and model the gospel to the next generation.

3. Teaching in the home needs to be both formal and informal.

4. We model the gospel most clearly by seeking and extending forgiveness.

➤ PRAY

Spend the next few minutes praying with and for one another.
Use the points below for guidance.

- Ask God to give you the discipline necessary to faithfully teach the next generation His Word.

- Pray that your marriage and the marriages in your church will be used by God to point the next generation to Christ.

- Pray that God will give you the grace to seek and extend forgiveness with your children.

READY TO LAUNCH
Family Action Plan

TEACHING THE GOSPEL

In Deuteronomy 6, the words we are supposed to teach to our children are His words—Scripture. Our own words will never have the same power that the Word of God has in the lives of our children. This is a great week to begin memorizing Scripture with your family. If you're not sure where to begin, you can start by picking a verse and taping it to the refrigerator. God's promise to us in Psalm 119 is that His Word will keep us from wandering and sinning against Him.

> *How can a young man keep his way pure?*
>
> *By guarding it according to your word.*
>
> *With my whole heart I seek you;*
>
> *let me not wander from your commandments!*
>
> *I have stored up your word in my heart,*
>
> *that I might not sin against you.*
>
> **PSALM 119:9-11**

Once you've chosen a verse, make a plan for how you'll accomplish this goal. Sweeten the deal with a reward when all your family members can recite the verse. This can be done many different ways. You could memorize one verse a week. You could dedicate a larger passage of Scripture to memory over the course of a few months. Or you could even purchase a CD with songs of Scripture to play at home or in the car. In our family, we're still humming Scripture that we listened to more than five years ago during our daily commute to school.

If you're still unsure where to begin, start with Psalm 119:9-11. With repetition, you can commit almost anything to memory. I'd bet your little one knows the words to all their favorite TV show theme songs. As our children have grown, turning the memory work into a game or competition always helps. It might even be time to dig out mnemonic devices from your own high school and college days. One favorite way is to use the first letter of each word as a reminder. Let your teenager write it on their hand and practice it any time they notice it during the day. Whatever you choose, any step toward memorizing part of the Bible is gaining ground.

Use the space below to map out a plan to start memorizing Scripture with your family.

_____

_____

_____

_____

_____

_____

_____

_____

_____

_____

_____

_____

_____

_____

_____

_____

_____

_____

_____

_____

➤ PERSONAL REFLECTION

God's Chosen Ones

> *Put on then, as God's chosen ones, holy and beloved,*
> *compassionate hearts, kindness, humility, meekness,*
> *and patience, bearing with one another and, if one has a*
> *complaint against another, forgiving each other, as the Lord*
> *has forgiven you, so you also must forgive.*
> **COLOSSIANS 3:12-13**

I (Jen) am a bit of a perfectionist. I like to get things right, preferably the first time without any mistakes. As the sole authority in our home most of the day (when my husband is at work), our four children present me with many opportunities to "get things right." I have the privilege of modeling the gospel as they make frequent mistakes. Unfortunately, I more often model guilt and fear instead of the gospel. Paul's encouragement to us in Colossians reminds me of several truths.

First, in our families, there's a need to "put on" compassion, kindness, humility and patience. I wonder if Paul ever had a future peek into my home. Sin runs rampant—in unfairness, unkindness, pride, and downright obnoxious behavior that tests my patience. Every home has opportunities to display the gospel in how we respond to our children's sin and foolishness.

Second, my job is to forgive as the Lord has forgiven me. That's a high calling. I struggle to say "I'm sorry" to our children when I make a mistake. For a genuinely careless mistake, "I'm sorry" will suffice, but many times what I am being called to do is much greater. Forgiveness is more costly. I need to put on humility once again and ask, "Please will you forgive me?" I must admit my sin (ouch!) and acknowledge how my own sin has damaged our relationship. I'm then asking for our relationship to be restored.

Do your children know the difference between "I'm sorry" and "Will you forgive me"?

What relationship most needs restoration right now in your home? What steps will you take toward restoration?

I want so much to believe I was right or justified in yelling, scolding, jumping to conclusions, reacting unfairly, or just plain trying to get my own way in our home. After all, I'm the parent. When my mistakes damage my relationships with my children, this is my opportunity to model the gospel and remind them of the forgiveness we've been given through a relationship with Jesus.

I often remind my children of the gospel prayer from J.D. Greear's book, *Gospel.* "In Christ, there is nothing I can do that would make You love me more, and nothing I have done that makes you love me less."[1] My mistakes don't change God's love toward me. And neither does theirs.

> *For I will be merciful toward their iniquities,*
>
> *and I will remember their sins no more.*
>
> **HEBREWS 8:12**

I'm so thankful God isn't a flawed parent like I am. He freely gives mercy and forgives sin. Because of the mercy and forgiveness we have received, we can also forgive. When we ask for forgiveness from our children, we model the gospel in front of them. In addition, when we graciously grant forgiveness to our children, we're reminding them God's forgiveness is available to them too.

In what ways do you struggle to remember their sins no more?

PERSONAL REFLECTION

God of Peace

> *What you have learned and received and heard and seen in me—*
> *practice these things, and the God of peace will be with you.*
>
> **PHILIPPIANS 4:9**

Growing up I (Will) was the second of four children. The first three were boys, and my sister was the youngest. We grew up in a home where my parents sought to put Christ first in everything and modeled for us what a godly marriage looked like. My siblings and I got along really well—for the most part.

There were times, however, when tempers would flare and emotions would run pretty hot. We were a competitive bunch, and none of us liked to lose. All four of us were pretty independent and wanted to chart our own course. This is precisely why it bothered me so much when my younger brother went through a phase when he emulated everything I did. He wanted to go with me wherever I went, play the same sports, and he even had the audacity to copy my Christmas list. Needless to say I wasn't too thrilled with him.

Now with many years behind me, I realize his behavior was normal, and I'm grateful for that season and the shared experiences with my brother. I also realize that we all emulate someone, whether it be a sibling, a sports hero, a boss, or church leader.

Paul knew this all too well, which is why he challenged the church at Philippi to imitate him. Paul was integral in starting the church, and as he writes from prison in Rome, he reminds them to "practice" the things they have learned, received, and heard from him. Simply put he's saying, "Follow my example!"

"Follow my example" is exactly what we should say to our children. We ought to set an example for the next generation in how to repent, seek forgiveness, study God's Word, engage in the local church, work, treat our spouse, pray, engage in the mission, and so much more. By doing so we help them to see the impact Christ has on our lives and further build their confidence in Him—our true and greater example.

What are specific ways you're modeling the gospel for your children?

Are there things that you are modeling for your children that aren't healthy? If so, what?

What are some things you desire to model for your children but currently are not?

1. J.D. Greear, *Gospel* (Nashville: B&H Books, 2011), 44.

GOD'S TWO GARDENS

HEBREWS 10:23-25

PROVERBS

As a middle school boy, I (David) was obnoxious and self-absorbed. Most middle school boys are. Despite my reluctance to take a shower or pay attention to anything other than the soccer field, an older teenager began investing in me when we met at church camp. For the next four years, Chris led a Bible study for me and my friends and walked alongside me through high school. We were a part of each other's weddings, we served together in ministry, and he even walked with me through becoming a father.

Chris modeled what it looked like to invest in someone's life, and he showed me the value of being connected to a community of believers. When I became a student pastor, I tried to do the same thing for students, showing up in the cafeteria or in the bleachers of their baseball games. As a parent now, I want to give that same gift to our children by seeking out and encouraging others to pour into our children's lives.

When our oldest daughter was old enough to participate in our church's student ministry, I was both excited and humbled. I was excited because I knew we were choosing for her a community where she could belong. We were intentionally seeking to make it the place she calls home, not the place where she feels like she's visiting. I was humbled because I knew we were reaching a season where many others would have more influence on her than we would. It was an exciting day when one of her leaders from church visited her at lunch during school. I remember the impact that had on my life, and we see the impact those relationships are having on our kids.

I've come to realize I want to build community for our younger children as early as we can. It can start with babysitters, Sunday morning teachers, nursery workers, our small group friends, or other adults at church who can help us drive the gospel deep. As Proverbs 24:6 says, "for by wise guidance you can wage your war, and in abundance of counselors there is victory."

As parents, we need the help. As believers, we have the opportunity to get help right in front of us.

➤ START

Share your Family Action Plan experience with memorizing Scripture from the past week.

Who was an adult who had a positive influence on you during your childhood? How were your actions, attitude, or faith affected by their influence?

➤ WATCH

GOAL: To communicate that God gives us two primary environments to raise our children: Home and Church.

VIDEO HIGHLIGHTS:

1. God intends the church to be a "second" family. We must prioritize the development of relationships in the church just as we do our homes.

2. Your children will feel like they "belong" certain places and are "visitors" at others. They'll imitate the people wherever they feel they belong. It's your job as a parent to make sure they "belong" at the right places.

3. This session will answer one of the most important questions you'll ever ask as a parent: "How should we define success?"

Watch Session 3: *God's Two Gardens*.
Use the notes page to record key quotes and ideas that stand out to you.

NOTES

→ DISCUSS

In his book, *Parenting Beyond Your Capacity*, Reggie Joiner wrote, "Children need more than just a family that gives them unconditional acceptance and love; they need a tribe that gives them a sense of belonging and significance."[1] The church should walk beside parents and help drive the gospel deep into the next generation.

> *Let us hold fast the confession of our hope without wavering, for he who promised is faithful. And let us consider how to stir up one another to love and good works, not neglecting to meet together, as is the habit of some, but encouraging one another, and all the more as you see the Day drawing near.*
>
> **HEBREWS 10:23-25**

Unfortunately, "more than two-thirds of young, churchgoing adults in America drop out of church between the ages of eighteen and twenty-two."[2] However, when high school students have two to five people (other than parents) regularly invest in their lives, they are up to twice as likely to stay engaged in the local church.[3] Our children need godly men and women who will faithfully encourage, mentor, teach, and even rebuke them. Such investment will go a long way toward developing a generation of fully devoted followers of Christ.

Are you currently investing in children other than your own? If so, what kind of impact have you had on their lives?

Are there currently adults, besides you and your spouse, who invest in the lives of your children? If so, what kind of impact have you seen in your children's lives?

Read the following verses on the importance of godly influence from the Book of Proverbs:

Where there is no guidance, a people falls, but in an abundance of counselors there is safety.

PROVERBS 11:14

The way of a fool is right in his own eyes, but a wise man listens to advice.

PROVERBS 12:15

By insolence comes nothing but strife, but with those who take advice is wisdom.

PROVERBS 13:10

Whoever walks with the wise becomes wise, but the companion of fools will suffer harm.

PROVERBS 13:20

The ear that listens to life-giving reproof will dwell among the wise. Whoever ignores instruction despises himself, but he who listens to reproof gains intelligence. The fear of the Lord is instruction in wisdom, and humility comes before honor.

PROVERBS 15:31-33

Listen to advice and accept instruction, that you may gain wisdom in the future.

PROVERBS 19:20

For by wise guidance you can wage your war, and in abundance of counselors there is victory.

PROVERBS 24:6

Oil and perfume make the heart glad, and the sweetness of a friend comes from his earnest counsel.

PROVERBS 27:9

How would you summarize the teaching in these verses? What are the common themes you observe?

It's important for you to surround your children with godly men and women who can speak truth and wisdom into their lives. This should come from their biological family and your church as well. The church is your family. We have the same inheritance. We have the same last name. We have the same history. We have the same future. And because of what Jesus did for us, we have the same Dad.

Only let your manner of life be worthy of the gospel of Christ, so that whether I come and see you or am absent, I may hear of you that you are standing firm in one spirit, with one mind striving side by side for the faith of the gospel, and not frightened in anything by your opponents. This is a clear sign to them of their destruction, but of your salvation, and that from God.

PHILIPPIANS 1:27-28

In these verses we learn what it means for the church to be a tight-knit family. Paul is writing this letter in prison trying to convince the church in Phillipi that if they don't stick together like family they are going to be overrun by the Romans. Paul is pleading with them for unity.

How does caring for the children in your church ultimately bring unity to the church?

Who are the godly men and women you would like to see take a greater role in investing in your child's life?

In the video, J.D. mentioned that children need a stable environment that's relationship heavy. But often we work to ensure that our children have great experiences at the cost of allowing time for others to invest in their lives.

What experiences competing for your time right now should you say "no" to in order to prioritize intentional relationships for your children?

What are some informal ways you can have others invest in your child's life?

In the video Veronica quoted Proverbs 13:20 and said, "Show me your friends and I'll show you your future."

Are you concerned about the friends your children currently have? If so, what steps do you need to take to intervene?

What questions do you have about discussing this with your child?

If you are single or married without children, how do Philippians 1:27-28 and the other passages in Proverbs shape the way you think about investing in the next generation?

What in your life needs to change in order to make room for investing in the next generation?

➤ WRAP-UP

1. There are two gardens that God uses to grow a child, the home and the church.

2. Parents can't overvalue experiences at the expense of having others form intentional relationships with their children.

3. In order for the next generation to thrive spiritually they need godly men and women other than their parents to invest in and mentor them.

➤ PRAY

Spend the next few minutes praying with and for one another. Use the points below for guidance.

- Ask God to bring godly, wise adults to invest in your child's life.

- Pray that God would give your children wisdom as they choose and make friends.

- Ask God to give you wisdom as you speak into the relationships your children are building.

Family Action Plan

THE FAMILY CALENDAR

Advance planning only comes naturally to a small percentage of people. Most of us have to be intentional at working on our scheduling skills.

Let's look at the calendar …

Start by making a calendar of an average week or month. It doesn't need to be fancy. A ruler, a pencil, and the space provided on the next page are all you need! The important thing is that you use a pencil so you can edit in the future. After all, this is a working calendar that needs to have room for God to grow your family and change your plans along the way.

Add in all things that affect your family time—when parents leave and arrive from work, sports, activities, and especially your commitments to the local church. Add in small group, weekend worship, and service opportunities.

What parts of your week are non-negotiable?

Could you add a family night each week where you say "no" to other invitations or activities in order to say "yes" to driving the gospel deep? Write out a plan for adding a family night in the space provided.

What kind of time are you currently investing in the local church? Who would you like to invite to spend time with your family or with one of your children? Could you schedule time with one of those people in the coming weeks? These are all questions you can schedule in the family calendar you create.

For this exercise to be most effective you have to keep doing it over and over again, each week or month. Again, for some people this will be really easy. But for those who are shaking their heads and contemplating tearing this page out of the book—stay the course and keep up the good work!

Use the space below to start your family calendar.

➤ # PERSONAL REFLECTION

Sending the Wrong Messages

> *Look carefully then how you walk, not as unwise but as wise,*
> *making the best use of the time, because the days are evil.*
> **EPHESIANS 5:15-16**

Parents and families in our culture are too busy. J.D. used the term *secondhand stress* in our video teaching time this week to describe what's happening to children as parents fill up their days and weeks with experiences that they believe will enrich their kids' lives instead of allowing their children unstructured time to play and rest. Parents are swamped, rushed and overwhelmed and it rubs off on the children in their presence. In his book, *Crazy Busy*, Kevin DeYoung writes,

> *"It's harder to ruin our kids than we think and harder to*
> *stamp them for success than we'd like. We fear that a few*
> *wrong moves will ruin our children forever, and at the same*
> *time assume that the right combination of protection and*
> *instruction will invariably produce godly children. ... By*
> *trying to do so much for them, we are actually making our*
> *kids less happy."*[4]

Are you aware of any secondhand stress you may be passing on to your children? What motivations or actions in your life do you need to reevaluate that may be sending wrong messages to your children?

One of the definitions of *stress* is "the burden on one's emotional or mental well-being created by demands on one's time."[5] I agree! Demands on our time cause a burden to our well-being. This is where I (Jen) need the reminder of Ephesians 5:15-16. There's not enough time in a day to accomplish everything I want to, so I must be wise in what I choose. The good news is my to-do list doesn't usually match up with God's list for me. I expect His list is shorter and has far more room in the calendar for rest. My husband would definitely agree. I'm more likely to be the one to fill the white space on our calendar with obligations. I've learned over time that the white space is most often where God works in and through us.

Is there something you're pursuing, either personally or for one of your children, that might not be on God's priority list for a wise use of your time?

Would you be willing to give that up? If not, what do you fear about losing that experience or opportunity?

➤ **PERSONAL REFLECTION**

Opening Up Your Life for Others

> *And let us consider how to stir up one another to love and good works, not neglecting to meet together, as is the habit of some, but encouraging one another, and all the more as you see the Day drawing near.*
>
> **HEBREWS 10:24-25**

When we look back on our lives we can see how our paths have intersected with people who've challenged us and shaped who we've become. Although painful at times, often it's for our good. Opening up our lives to someone isn't always an easy thing to do because we never know how people are going to respond when they begin to see what's underneath the surface.

God never intended us to go through life void of relationships. In fact, we see God's intent for relationships expressed in the "one anothers" found throughout Scripture, specifically the New Testament. Here are just a few examples:

> *A new commandment I give to you, that you love one another: just as I have loved you, you also are to love one another.*
>
> **JOHN 13:34**

> *Outdo one another in showing honor.*
>
> **ROMANS 12:10**

> *Live in harmony with one another.*
>
> **ROMANS 12:16**

Therefore welcome one another as Christ has welcomed you,
for the glory of God.

ROMANS 15:7

Bear one another's burdens.

GALATIANS 6:2

We see the "one anothers" modeled by the way Paul shared his life with others. Paul had close friends like Barnabas, who walked beside him as a co-laborer and Timothy, whom he was raising up to lead the next generation. Both played an integral role in Paul's life and he in theirs. Without these types of relationships, the "one anothers" of the Scriptures can't be lived out, and we won't develop into the parents God is leading us to be.

Whom have you asked to invest and speak intentionally into your life?

Besides your children, whom are you intentionally investing in?

What fears keep you from living out the *one anothers* of Scripture?

1. Reggie Joiner and Carey Nieuwhof, *Parenting Beyond Your Capacity: Connect Your Family to a Wider Community* (Colorado Springs: David C. Cook, 2010), 67.
2. Thom S. Rainer and Sam S. Rainer, *Essential Church?: Reclaiming a Generation of Dropouts* (Nashville: B&H, 2008), 2.
3. LifeWay Research, "Parents & Churches Can Help Teens Stay in Church," *LifeWay Research* Published August 7, 2007. Accessed April 22, 2014. *http://www.lifewayresearch.com/2007/08/07/parents-churches-can-help-teens-stay-in-church/*
4. Kevin DeYoung, *Crazy Busy* (Wheaton: Crossway, 2013), 68-71.
5. *Merriam Webster's Collegiate Dictionary*, 11th ed., s.v. "stress."

PREPARING OUR CHILDREN FOR GOD'S MISSION

MATTHEW 9:35-38

This year, we (David and Jen) gave our ten-year-old daughter a garden as a gift. It was only the promise of the garden in the form of a gardening book, since it wasn't springtime yet, but we figured that if we gave her the structure she could choose where, when, and what she wanted to plant. With her vision and the care of her seeds, our daughter's garden will produce a bountiful harvest. And she is thrilled.

For a ten-year-old, bountiful might only mean enough basil for one pizza or enough cucumbers for one summer snack, but she's driven by thinking of things we can harvest. She's imagining growing fresh herbs to season her dinner and growing cherry tomatoes she can offer to her sister. The process will be hard at times, but the end result will be what makes it worth the time and sweat.

You see, each seed contains a promise. The seeds she'll plant will grow into something so much more than a seed. And she gets to watch its transformation. The crops she'll harvest, no matter how small, will bring all of us great joy. And hopefully a full stomach for at least one meal.

Similarly, that's our unique role with children. We have the privilege of laboring to help them grow. Speaking to new Christians in Corinth, Paul writes in 1 Corinthians 3:6, "I planted, Apollos watered, but God gave the growth." Just like Paul, we don't do it alone. The church partners with us in preparing our children to be part of the mission of God. Our seeds require much care now, but their purpose is great.

➤ START

What did you learn from last week's activity that helped you make your calendar more intentional towards garden growing?

Relatively speaking, how tight is your grip on your children? In terms of living within culture today, would you say it's easy or difficult to trust God with your children?

➤ WATCH

GOAL: To communicate that God gives us children to prepare them for His mission.

VIDEO HIGHLIGHTS:

1. Our children, the next generation, are like arrows in the hand of a mighty warrior, which we launch out into the battle that God has set before them.

2. A safety-obsessed approach to parenting (i.e. "helicopter parenting") not only harms our children socially, it can turn them away from the faith.

3. Gospel-centered parenting isn't defined by a list of dos and don'ts. It's about capturing our children's heart for the mission of God.

4. Following Jesus is more likely to become a passion and obsession when we engage our children early in the mission of God.

Watch Session 4: *Preparing Our Children for God's Mission.*
Use the notes page to record key quotes and ideas that stand out to you.

NOTES

→ DISCUSS

With the birth of every child comes the hopes and dreams of what they'll one day become. Every major milestone is anticipated with more excitement than the one before. Yet with all the joy each milestone brings, it still doesn't answer the question every parent must ask: "Why has God given me children?" The answer to this question will dictate both how we raise our kids and what we teach them to value most.

Leading the next generation to set their hope in God requires preparing them to be launched into His mission. This certainly doesn't mean that God will call every child to Christian ministry or international missions. In fact, most won't. He'll call our children to everything from medicine to the arts and from business to academics. But regardless of their vocational calling, their mission remains the same—to make disciples! Jesus said, "Go therefore and make disciples of all nations, baptizing them in the name of the Father and of the Son and of the Holy Spirit, teaching them to observe all that I have commanded you. And behold, I am with you always, to the end of the age" (Matt. 28:19-20). The next generation of disciple-makers is in our homes, and we must prepare to send them out.

And Jesus went throughout all the cities and villages, teaching in their synagogues and proclaiming the gospel of the kingdom and healing every disease and every affliction. When he saw the crowds, he had compassion for them, because they were harassed and helpless, like sheep without a shepherd. Then he said to his disciples, "The harvest is plentiful, but the laborers are few; therefore pray earnestly to the Lord of the harvest to send out laborers into his harvest."

MATTHEW 9:35-38

Matthew described the crowds using vivid language like "harassed," "help-less," and "like a sheep without a shepherd" (v. 36). His description accurately describes the condition of our world today.

How can we help the next generation see the vast spiritual, physical, and emotional needs that exist today?

Scripture says that when Jesus saw the need "he had compassion for them" (v. 36). How do you define *compassion*?

What specifically did Jesus do to show compassion to the crowds? How does this encourage you to show compassion like Jesus? To whom does this encourage you to show compassion?

Jesus challenged His disciples to "pray earnestly to the Lord of the harvest to send out laborers into his harvest." How does this shape or change how you regularly pray for your children?

One effective way to prepare to send the next generation into His harvest is to engage them early in serving others. What opportunities exist for your family to serve in your church and local community?

In what ways are you actively helping your children think about their role in God's plan for reaching the nations?

Helping the next generation understand that God has a role for them to play in His grand story of the universe is critical to capturing their heart. In *Parenting Beyond Your Capacity*, Reggie Joiner wrote, "When there is nothing more challenging or adventurous about your style of faith, you begin to drift toward other things that seem more interesting and meaningful."[1]

What are some trappings the next generation might find more "interesting and meaningful" than their role in God's story?

Jim Elliot, a missionary serving natives in Ecuador, died as a martyr in 1956. Before he died, he wrote in his journal, "He is no fool who gives what he cannot keep to gain what he cannot lose."[2] Spend some time encouraging one another how to help children see that the blessings of Christ far outweigh the things of this world.

➤ WRAP-UP

1. God has given us children to prepare them for His mission.

2. Preparing the next generation involves engaging them in the church, locally, and globally.

3. Without an appropriate understanding of their role in God's grand story the next generation will drift toward things they think are more meaningful.

➤ PRAY

**Spend the next few minutes praying with and for one another.
Use the points below for guidance.**

- Pray for God to give you and your children a passion and a love for people who don't know Him.

- Pray that God would raise up each of your children to send into His harvest regardless of where that might be.

- Pray that God would keep the next generation from falling into the trappings of this world.

- Pray for wisdom to rightly convey the truth that in the presence of Christ there is "fullness of joy; at your right hand are pleasures forevermore" (Ps. 16:11).

Family Action Plan

THE ACTS 1:8 STRATEGY

This exercise will lead you in developing an Acts 1:8 strategy for your family to be part of God's mission for sharing the gospel with the world.

Before Jesus ascended into heaven, He left His disciples this mission strategy.

> *But you will receive power when the Holy Spirit has come upon you, and you will be my witnesses in Jerusalem and in all Judea and Samaria, and to the end of the earth.*
>
> **ACTS 1:8**

We are His mission strategy! It's humbling to know God uses us to minister to people when He could easily display His power without us.

List your local spheres of influence—your Jerusalem. These are the comfortable places where you already belong: schools, neighborhoods, teams, and community organizations. Circle one group your family can serve in a tangible way.

Name an area or people group in your city you are intrigued by, curious about, or interested in serving. For the disciples, going into Judea and Samaria was uncomfortable. This group of people may be close by, but out of your comfort zone.

Discuss the possibility of connecting with a country or unreached people group. Your plan may be easier to fulfill if you choose an area that your church already has a relationship with. Brainstorm and list ways you might be able to serve that country.

After our (David and Jen) oldest daughter's first mission trip, we decided to sponsor a girl through Compassion International from that same country. There are many Christian organizations that allow you the opportunity to sponsor a child. Writing letters to Maciel has given our kids a glimpse into how privileged we are in the United States and how the gospel transcends all of our differences. We've also had great conversations stem from watching Operation World videos. They've worked well in helping our family know how to pray for the countries we know nothing about.

The chart below is to help you make a strategic plan for exposing and engaging your children in the mission of God. For the first month, try researching your family's areas. Watch videos on the Internet, gather information, reach out to a neighbor, and spend time praying for those areas of focus. In the coming months, look for ways to stretch yourself. Your family will follow your lead.

Acts 1:8 Strategy	Your Family's Area	This Month	In Six Months	This Year
Jerusalem				
Judea and Samaria				
Ends of the Earth				

➤ PERSONAL REFLECTION

Your Child's Part in God's Story

> *Let no one despise you for your youth, but set the believers*
> *an example in speech, in conduct, in love, in faith, in purity.*
> **1 TIMOTHY 4:12**

Over and over in the Bible, God chooses to use the unexpected to accomplish His purposes and glorify His name.

- Because of Miriam's courage, she was used by God to preserve Moses' life as an infant (Ex. 2:4-8).

- Joshua began serving Moses in his youth (Num. 11:28).

- Saul discredited David's potential in his battle against Goliath because he was young and small (1 Sam. 17:33). Boy, was he wrong!

- Josiah began to seek God as a teenage king and began to purge his nation of idol worship (2 Chron. 34:3-7).

- When God gave Jeremiah a word to preach, Jeremiah couldn't believe he was old enough for people to listen (Jer. 1:4-9). God didn't let that stop him.

- Daniel was able to resist assimilation into Babylonian culture as a teenager and received favor from the king that led to his leadership for many years (Dan. 1:3-16).

- Mary was chosen to be Jesus' mother as an unwed teenager (Luke 1:26-35).

Do any of these stories remind you of your children?

Most teenagers don't exemplify gracious speech, perfect conduct, unconditional love, unwavering faith and total purity. Neither did the youth of the Bible. We know God sees the hearts of our children and yet still chooses to give us the words of 1 Timothy 4:12.

God's plan is to use your children, no matter their age. There are parts they can play in watching the story of God's rescue and redemption unfold.

Is it comforting or frightening to you that God plans to use your children in His story of rescue and redemption?

How could you specifically encourage each of your children this week that they can play a part in the mission of God? Look to your family's Acts 1:8 strategy for potential opportunities.

➤ PERSONAL REFLECTION

Giving Your Child to God

> *For this child I prayed, and the LORD has granted me my*
> *petition that I made to him. Therefore I have lent him to the*
> *LORD. As long as he lives, he is lent to the LORD.*
>
> **1 SAMUEL 1:27-28**

We all have dreams—dreams for our careers, homes, relationships, and, of course, our children. What do you dream for yours? Do you dream they will be academically gifted and graduate with highest honors? Do you dream they'll find a spouse, be happily married and have lots of grandchildren for you to love and spoil? If you're a Christian, it's likely you have big dreams that God would do great things for His kingdom through your children!

First Samuel tells us the story of Hannah. While yet childless, Hannah vowed to the Lord that should He bless her with a son, she would "give him to the LORD all the days of his life" (1 Sam. 1:11). Scripture continues to tell us that she did bear a son. And as soon as she was able, Hannah brought her son, Samuel, before the priests. Some versions of the Bible use the term *give* rather than *lent* in 1 Samuel 1:27-28. The term *give* seems to carry more weight, and perhaps seems a bit more permanent.

If the primary purpose of having children is to prepare them for God's mission, wouldn't we all be wise to have the same mindset and attitude as Hannah? Isn't the willingness to "let go" the first step toward allowing God to use your children? As a mom, I (Julie) can't imagine taking my young child to the nearest church and leaving him there!

Perhaps you're thinking, *Of course we want God to use our children to do whatever is needed to build His kingdom! What a privilege that would be!* But have you seriously considered the what-ifs? What if that meant they were called into full-time ministry? "That's no big deal," you say. What if it meant that full-time ministry took them to a foreign land? What about a *hostile* foreign land? What if it meant they would have an incurable disease, but that would allow them an incredible platform through which they could share the gospel? Does it still sound so great?

Remember, according to Psalm 127, children are like "arrows in the hand of a warrior." For an arrow to be launched, it must be released. So too we must release our children to the perfect plans of God, knowing He cares for them far more than we do.

What dreams do you have for your children in their futures?

How are you actively preparing your children to engage in His mission?

Releasing our children to God like Hannah can be really hard. What are you most afraid of and why?

1. Reggie Joiner and Carey Nieuwhof, *Parenting Beyond Your Capacity: Connect Your Family to a Wider Community* (Colorado Springs: David C. Cook, 2010), 184.
2. Elisabeth Elliot, *Shadow of the Almighty* (New York: Harper Collins, 1958), 15.

DISCIPLINE: FIGHT FOR THE HEART

HEBREWS 12:3-11

"Mommmmmm, I need your help!"

It always happens when I (Jen) am stirring something finicky on the stove or getting ready to walk out the door. Those words come ringing through the house. Whether it's a yo-yo string, a head full of tangled hair, a jewelry chain, a first grader's shoelaces, or a long division problem, I'm willing to untangle it, even if I do it grumbling as I'm chasing kids out the front door for soccer practice.

I secretly love the challenge of untangling a big mess. It might be the only tangible thing I accomplish in a day besides doing laundry and cooking dinner. Most recently it was a light-up toy ball on an elastic string, a coveted birthday party favor that keeps coming back out of the toy chest. As I narrowly missed getting hit in the face with it in the front hallway, I noticed the tangle. All the kids had ignored the knot, and I suggested we work on getting it out. Picking apart each tiny knot took almost half an hour, but when I was done, it was as good as new.

Hebrews 12:1 says, "Therefore, since we are surrounded by so great a cloud of witnesses, let us also lay aside every weight, and sin which clings so closely, and let us run with endurance the race that is set before us." We know our own sin entangles us, but do we believe that about the hearts of our children? One of our jobs as parents is to work slowly and diligently to untangle them from their sin and free them to run the race God has prepared for them. We do that by deliberately choosing to move past our children's actions to examine their hearts. We have the privilege of not only disciplining our children but training them to race toward righteousness.

They'll never run far with tangled shoelaces, so let's get started.

➤ START

What area of your Acts 1:8 strategy is your family most looking forward to?

What is the most creative discipline you've either employed or seen used in your years of parenting?

➤ WATCH

GOAL: To communicate that godly discipline is a fight for the hearts of the next generation.

VIDEO HIGHLIGHTS:

1. When it comes to discipline, the world is primarily focused on coercing behavior, whereas the gospel focuses on changing the heart.

2. Many approaches to discipline foster idolatry rather than combat it. This has eternal consequences.

3. In discipline, combat the 3 D's: dishonesty, disrespect, and disobedience.

Watch Session 5: *Discipline: Fight for the Heart.*
Use the notes page to record key quotes and ideas that stand out to you.

NOTES

Changing the Heart
fight for your Kids not w/Kids

Discipline - Psalm 27 - fight for the heart
Reshape the Heart - Love what God Loves,
& - If you behave - Than you get Reward
Change Heart but not by Reward.
Primary Focus Honoring God.
Disrespect, Dishonesty & Disobedience
Noone w/ these 3 things ever turn
out well, if you don't address this

Don't Be Lazy. Teach them to
obey. Take the time even when
tired. "Go to Bed" to Lazy to get
up to enforce. All the Way, Right away.
with a happy Heart.
Be Swift to discipline & bring
back for fellowship.

Pray alot for guidance

➤ DISCUSS

Disciplining our children is one of the most difficult aspects of parenting. Sometimes it feels easier just to avoid it! However, without loving discipline, our children will never learn what it means to live in right relationship with God, others, and even themselves. Our goal in discipline must move beyond changing their behavior and toward changing the desires of their hearts. This begins with understanding that behind every behavioral sin is a self-centered motivation. Our challenge is to help our children consistently identify the self-centered motives behind their behavior. We discipline by fighting for their hearts.

Consider him who endured from sinners such hostility against himself, so that you may not grow weary or fainthearted. In your struggle against sin you have not yet resisted to the point of shedding your blood. And have you forgotten the exhortation that addresses you as sons?

"My son, do not regard lightly the discipline of the Lord, nor be weary when reproved by him. For the Lord disciplines the one he loves, and chastises every son whom he receives."

It is for discipline that you have to endure. God is treating you as sons. For what son is there whom his father does not discipline? If you are left without discipline, in which all have participated, then you are illegitimate children and not sons. Besides this, we have had earthly fathers who disciplined us and we respected them. Shall we not much more be subject to the Father of spirits and live? For they disciplined us for a short time as it seemed best to them, but he disciplines us for our good, that we may share his holiness. For the moment all discipline seems painful rather than pleasant, but later it yields the peaceful fruit of righteousness to those who have been trained by it.

HEBREWS 12:3-11

The author of Hebrews begins this teaching on discipline by first reminding us to "consider" what Christ has done. Why does this take first priority in our discipline?

One of the explicit challenges of this passage is not to "regard lightly" or "be weary" (v. 5) of God's discipline in our lives. In what ways are you teaching and leading your children to regard and embrace your discipline?

Scripture says that "the Lord disciplines the one he loves" (v. 6). How are you working to ensure that your children recognize your discipline as love?

The way to lead our children to change their desires is to show them the beauty and majesty of Jesus! Thomas Chalmers wrote, "The only way to dispossess the heart of an old affection is by the expulsive power of a new one."[1] We must constantly help the next generation see that Jesus truly is better and worthy of their lives, of which godly discipline plays a vital role. In fact, this is precisely what God does in the life of every believer.

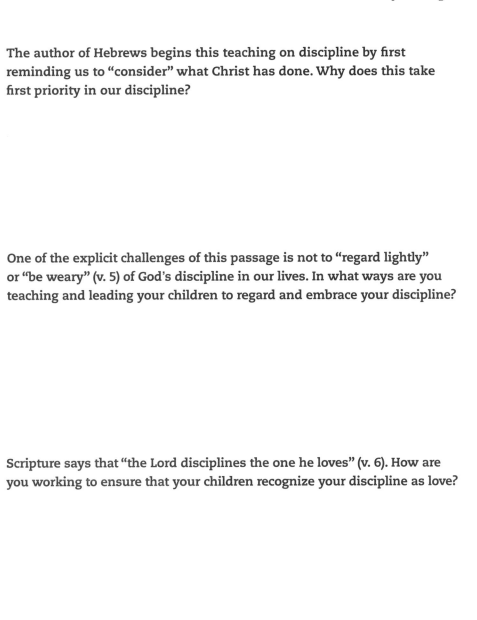

God is constantly in the process of disciplining us. Do you find it difficult to be consistent in the discipline of your children? If so, why?

Verse 10 says that God disciplines us "for our good, that we may share his holiness." What does this mean, and how does it motivate you?

What does the writer of Hebrews say are the results of godly discipline in the last sentence of this passage? Is this encouraging? Why or why not?

➤ WRAP-UP

1. Parents are the means through which God disciplines children.

2. Godly discipline is a fight for the hearts of the next generation.

3. Behind every behavioral sin is a self-centered desire that needs to be replaced with a desire for Christ.

4. Godly discipline is an act of love.

➤ PRAY

Spend the next few minutes praying with and for one another. Use the points below for guidance.

- Pray that God would give you the wisdom to clearly see what's motivating your children (the sin behind the sin).

- Ask God to show you the most effective ways to discipline your children with their hearts ultimately in mind.

- Ask God for courage to discipline well even though the path of least resistance is to do nothing.

READY TO LAUNCH
Family Action Plan

THE FAMILY DISCIPLINE PLAN

In Ezekiel, we see what we need to change behaviors. God said,

> *And I will give you a new heart, and a new spirit I will put within you. And I will remove the heart of stone from your flesh and give you a heart of flesh. And I will put my Spirit within you, and cause you to walk in my statutes and be careful to obey my rules.*
>
> **EZEKIEL 36:26-27**

Our behaviors point to our idols, the very things that are pulling us away from a joyful pursuit of our Heavenly Father and turning our hearts to stone. Instead of using our children's idols to coerce them into behavior that makes us look like good parents, let's pursue how we can replace the lies we believe with the truth of the gospel.

Take some time to jot down difficult or disobedient behaviors you see in your children. After writing them down, hide the list if necessary. The goal isn't to highlight weaknesses, but to build our children up with the truth of God's Word. Do you have appropriate, clearly communicated consequences for the behaviors you listed? If not, this is the week to set some up!

Many parents would agree it's extremely difficult to be consistent in our discipline. Sometimes we're too harsh, and other times, we ignore the very same thing that had us red-faced and yelling the day before. Our hope is that this tool is one you can use again and again as you set consequences for behavior in your home. We've given examples, but allowed space for you to use as it fits your family.

BEHAVIOR	SELF-CENTERED DESIRE	TRUTH	CONSEQUENCE	THIS YEAR
Direct Disobedience	I want to do things my way.	Colossians 3:20		
Lying		Psalm 25:1; Proverbs 12:22		
Disrespect		Exodus 20:12		
"Out of Control"		Proverbs 25:28; Philippians 4:13		
Complaining or whining about responsibilities		Ephesians 6:7		

Share with your family that you'd like to establish some guidelines to help you be consistent in your discipline. Tell them what you're learning during your small-group study. Remind them of the grace we have all been given in Jesus. You will be off to a great start at seeing the gospel transform their behaviors.

➤ # PERSONAL REFLECTION

Modeling Holiness

> *Therefore lift your drooping hands and strengthen your weak knees, and make straight paths for your feet, so that what is lame may not be put out of joint but rather be healed. Strive for peace with everyone, and for the holiness without which no one will see the Lord. See to it that no one fails to obtain the grace of God; that no "root of bitterness" springs up and causes trouble, and by it many become defiled; that no one is sexually immoral or unholy like Esau, who sold his birthright for a single meal. For you know that afterward, when he desired to inherit the blessing, he was rejected, for he found no chance to repent, though he sought it with tears.*
>
> **HEBREWS 12:12-17**

These verses follow an exhortation that discipline, while unpleasant at the time, produces the fruit of righteousness. The word *discipline* conjures up a negative mental image for many parents. They picture harsh punishment or unfair correction. And yes, most discipline is unpleasant and inconvenient. But it doesn't always have to be so.

What images does the word *discipline* bring to your mind?

Our discipline toward our children is part of their discipleship, us training them in how to be more like Christ. Training involves recognizing our children's sin, calling it out, and reminding them that God's way is much better. Most often, that is an action instead of a reaction. Action requires me to lift my drooping hands and strengthen my weak knees. In doing so, my discipline can move from harsh to gentle, from unfair to just. It moves from punishment to intentional training. It moves from correction to discipleship.

So, I (Jen) first take these verses as a personal challenge to seek holiness. In doing that, my children will have the opportunity to "see the Lord." As the airlines usually say, put on your own oxygen mask first before you assist the children around you. Being connected to Jesus first gives me the chance to make a straight path my children can follow.

Second, I see these verses as a warning. How sad it must have been for Isaac and Rebekah to see Esau miss the blessing of his birthright. I neither want my children to fail to obtain the grace of God nor miss a blessing that God intends, and find themselves tearfully seeking it when it's too late.

Do your children see you reading your Bible, accepting and acknowledging God's discipline in your own life, seeking holiness, avoiding bitterness, and striving for peace?

What would happen if your children began to see this consistency in your life?

PERSONAL REFLECTION

Avoid the Crippling Effect of Fear

> *For I know the plans I have for you, declares the LORD, plans for welfare and not for evil, to give you a future and a hope. Then you will call upon me and come and pray to me, and I will hear you. You will seek me and find me, when you seek me with all your heart.*
>
> **JEREMIAH 29:11-13**

Many parents deal with crippling fears regarding the future and well-being of their children. I (Julie) recently made some new friends, and it wasn't long before our conversation turned to our kids. Both of these women had sons older than my children. Each had a son who was preparing to move away to college within the next two years. When I asked one of them where her son was hoping to go, she opened up about her fears of him attending the Naval Academy. She was scared to have him so far away—in the military. The other mom quickly chimed in about how fearful she was that her son would turn away from God when he went off to school, despite the fact that he was brought up in a Christian home with godly values. She feared his faith might not be "his own."

Often times we allow our fears to shape the way we discipline. Our fears can lead us to discipline too harshly as we try to "control" our kids. At other times, we can become passive in our discipline because we fear pushing our children away. However, we must remember that God uses the discipline of parents to shape the trajectory of our children and push them to Christ.

As parents we must combat our fears by claiming the promises of God found in Scripture. Promises that remind us God has plans for our children that are for their good and for His glory. Promises like those found in Isaiah 43:1-2. "But now thus says the LORD, he who created you, O Jacob, he who formed you, O Israel: 'Fear not, for I have redeemed you; I have called you by name, you are mine. When you pass through the waters, I will be with you; and through the rivers, they shall not overwhelm you; when you walk through fire you shall not be burned, and the flame shall not consume you.'"

His desires for our children are even better than anything we could imagine! His desires are brought to reality through the faithful shepherding and disciplining of parents. It's a hard job, but God promises that the trials of parenthood will not overcome us!

What are your biggest fears as a parent?

What do your fears reveal about your trust in God? Are there areas where you need to repent of a lack of faith?

What promises of God do you need to claim today as you seek to faithfully parent your children?

1. Thomas Chalmers, *The Expulsive Power of a New Affection* (Minneapolis: Curiosmith, 2012), 19.

DISCIPLINE: FIGHT FOR YOUR KIDS, NOT WITH YOUR KIDS

EPHESIANS 6:1-4

COLOSSIANS 3:21

PSALM 4:4-5

"Same team, Michael. Same team!"

When our (David and Jen) son began playing recreational soccer, we were proud parents. Because it was his first season, we filmed every game. In every video, the coach's voice can be heard booming above the rest, reminding one player that he was part of a team.

The boys were only three years old, but they already loved to win. Another player, Michael, constantly took the ball away from our son. Really, Michael was faster and better than all of the other players, so he scored 99.9% of the goals. You can imagine our son's devastation that soccer didn't involve him scoring 99.9% of the goals. The devastation usually showed up in tears and tantrums. It was a season worth filming.

Michael needed a constant reminder that there was no need to steal the ball from his teammates. They were on the same team, scoring in the same goal, collecting the same points!

Our children need a frequent reminder that we are on their team, working with them toward the same goal. We need the same reminder as parents. I'm often surprised when one of our children sins against us or against someone in our family. I shouldn't be. Their sinful behaviors and choices are the result of a sinful heart. I know Satan is waging war on our families and we need to fight together against our sin.

When they fight the temptation to sin and reap the sometimes devastating consequences of their sin, we are there to fight with them, pick them up and stand up with them again to work toward the next goal.

Same team, Mom and Dad! Same team!

➤ START

Have you put into practice any of your consequences from last session's discipline plan? How did it go?

As you look back on the previous sessions, what lesson or activity has been most fruitful for your family?

➤ WATCH

GOAL: To communicate a constructive approach to discipline centered on love and hope instead of anger.

VIDEO HIGHLIGHTS:

1. We must never discipline our children out of personal vengeance, but out of love because we want them to become everything God has planned for them to be.

2. Discipline isn't just a "big idea;" we need practical suggestions. This session will provide some.

3. The Enemy wants to discipline your kids as well, but he does it in a fundamentally different way than the gospel instructs us to do it.

Watch Session 6: *Discipline: Fight for Your Kids, Not with Your Kids.*
Use the notes page to record key quotes and ideas that stand out to you.

NOTES

➤ DISCUSS

At the end of the Book of Revelation the apostle John gives us a vision for what awaits every person who hopes in Christ. He paints a picture of a new heaven and a new earth where God restores all things and reigns as our King. It's a promise that resonates in the heart of every believer and a hope that won't disappoint. Knowing that Christ has gone before us to prepare our eternal dwelling serves as a wonderful motivation to persevere and stay the course.

Just as we need a vision of the future to encourage us, our children also need us to continue holding before them a vision of the man or woman God is leading them to become. Casting this vision, in part, requires us to faithfully discipline our children. Paul David Tripp said, "[Y]ou discipline your child because you want that child to begin to embrace the depth of their sin, and therefore, the depth of their need, and therefore, hunger for the Lord Jesus Christ."[1] With this in mind it's good to consider how we discipline our children.

> *Children, obey your parents in the Lord, for this is right. "Honor your father and mother" (this is the first commandment with a promise), "that it may go well with you and that you may live long in the land." Fathers, do not provoke your children to anger, but bring them up in the discipline and instruction of the Lord.*
>
> **EPHESIANS 6:1-4**

> *Fathers, do not provoke your children, lest they become discouraged.*
>
> **COLOSSIANS 3:21**

There are many ways parents can "provoke [their] children to anger" (Eph. 6:4), such as showing favoritism, creating unrealistic expectations, and overprotection. One way parents must constantly fight against provoking their children is to not discipline them out of anger.

Not disciplining out of anger is one of the challenges that every parent faces when they see the consequences of their child's sin. Why is this so difficult?

When you discipline out of anger what does it reveal about the condition of your heart in the moment?

> *Be angry, and do not sin;*
>
> *ponder in your own hearts on your beds, and be silent.*
>
> *Offer right sacrifices,*
>
> *and put your trust in the LORD.*
>
> **PSALM 4:4-5**

In this psalm David challenges us to "Be angry, and do not sin" (Ps. 4:4). What does this teach us about the relationship between *anger* and *sin*?

What did David do to keep his anger from manifesting itself in sin?

What practical steps are you taking (or should take) to ensure your discipline isn't motivated by anger?

In the midst of disciplining your child, how can you speak a positive vision (instead of a guilt-motivated vision) of what God wants for them?

Would your children see you as someone who more often builds them up or criticizes them? Discuss.

Coming out of this discussion, what is one step you can take to change the way you discipline your children?

➤ WRAP-UP

1. Children need their parents to hold before them a biblical vision of the man or woman God longs for each of them to become.

2. Faithful discipline will help lead the next generation to spiritual maturity.

3. Parents must fight to discipline their children out of love and not anger.

➤ PRAY

**Spend the next few minutes praying with and for one another.
Use the points below for guidance.**

- Pray that God would give you a clear picture of the man or woman God is leading your child to become.

- Ask God for wisdom to know how to speak a biblical vision into your child's life.

- Pray that God would give you patience when disciplining your children in order to keep them from becoming discouraged.

- Ask God to let your words be used as a means to build up rather than criticize.

Family Action Plan

PRAYING HANDS

To begin, you'll need to either trace your own hand or the hands of your children onto a piece of paper or in the space provided on the next page. If your child's hand is small enough, we'd encourage you to trace your child's hand inside of your own. Use this as a reminder that you are praying over your child. Do this for each child and use it as prayer guide as you jot down notes within each finger. This is an opportunity to look back on some of the activities you have done and use what you've discovered as a way to pray specifically for each of your children.

THUMB. J.D. mentioned in the video that his father "held up a crown for him to grow into." How can you create a crown your child can grow into? What beautiful character qualities do you see being part of that crown? If you've asked God to show you a vision for who your children are becoming, pray for that vision to develop. Write down, inside the thumb or beside it, a specific goal you see God working on in them. This week, also take a chance to write them a note (if they can read) and share how you much you love them and how you see God working in them.

POINTER. How has God uniquely gifted your child? Ask them what they think. What is a quality of Jesus you see developing in them that you can pray for?

MIDDLE. Who is someone who stands "taller" than your child? Someone you'd like to see them emulate, learn from, or spend time with. This is a reminder to pray for opportunities for other people in our churches to invest in our children.

RING FINGER. This finger is the weakest, so jot down a struggle your child is facing. This might be the very thing that makes you forget all your good intentions with discipline. Fight with your kids against this sin by praying against it faithfully.

PINKY. The smallest finger can remind you that each of your children are part of God's bigger story in the world. Pray that your child will see no greater time than the present to engage in the mission of God.

Use the space provided below to complete the Praying Hands activity.

PERSONAL REFLECTION

Remember Whose You Are

> *Do not let your adorning be external—the braiding of hair and the putting on of gold jewelry, or the clothing you wear—but let your adorning be the hidden person of the heart with the imperishable beauty of a gentle and quiet spirit, which in God's sight is very precious.*
>
> **1 PETER 3:3-4**

Braids are my (Jen) favorite hairstyle. In fact, I forced my two daughters to be my guinea pigs for an entire summer as I learned how to French braid. I'm not very good or fast, but I can do it. Nothing beats two French braids for a summer hairstyle. As often as I beg the girls to let me braid their hair, I should more often encourage them to be adorned with a gentle and quiet spirit.

We live in a society that overemphasizes external beauty, particularly in women. It becomes evident, even in elementary school, that girls will struggle to believe that beauty comes from the heart. My first responsibility is to believe that truth for myself so I can pass it on to my daughters.

How does it make you feel to know you're beautiful and precious to God?

My second responsibility is to pass on to our daughters that they, too, are beautiful and precious to God. As I set a vision for what I want to see our daughters become, I imagine a crown studded with biblical virtues: things unseen but precious to God.

Qualities like:

- Generosity – 1 Timothy 6:18-19
- Perseverance – Hebrews 12:1
- Humility – 1 Peter 5:5
- Contentment – Philippians 4:12-13
- Love for God's Word – Psalm 119:10
- Purity – Psalm 51:10

"Remember whose you are." A friend of mine often reminds her daughters of that phrase when they leave her care, whether to go overnight or just to school. It's a short reminder for a continual discussion that we are children of God. Bought and adopted at a high price. Precious and beloved. Designed to reflect Him. That's the kind of crown I want to set up for our children to grow into.

What jewels would be on the crown you would you have your children grow up into?

How can you speak that vision over them this week?

➤ PERSONAL REFLECTION

Lead Like Jesus

> *Do nothing from selfish ambition or conceit, but in humility*
> *count others more significant than yourselves. Let each*
> *of you look not only to his own interests, but also to the*
> *interests of others. Have this mind among yourselves, which*
> *is yours in Christ Jesus.*
>
> **PHILIPPIANS 2:3-5**

Words can't adequately express how thankful I (Will) am for my earthly father. My father set an incredible example and taught my siblings and me what it means to be a leader. He taught us great leadership principles ranging from developing a strong work ethic, owning our mistakes, dealing with conflict, to becoming people of character. However, what stuck with me the most is the servant posture my father took in every relationship. This is exemplified to this day in the way he serves his wife, employer, co-workers, friends, and his kids. He's always striving to put the needs of others above his own and therefore proclaim the love of Christ and the power of the gospel.

In Mark 10 Jesus was approached by James and John, who made an audacious request: "Grant us to sit, one at your right hand and one at your left, in your glory" (v. 37). What Jesus taught next would teach us all an incredibly valuable lesson on leadership.

> *But it shall not be so among you. But whoever would be*
> *great among you must be your servant, and whoever would*
> *be first among you must be slave of all. For even the Son of*
> *Man came not to be served but to serve, and to give his life*
> *as a ransom for many.*
>
> **MARK 10:43-45**

Now I'm the father of four children (one daughter and three boys), and I pray that God would use me to teach and model for my children what it means to be a godly man, not only in what I say but what I do. We all realize however that this is so much easier said than done! Daily I find myself short-tempered, driven by self-centered desires, and pushing to have things done "my way." Perhaps you feel the same way.

Our only hope in combating our self-centeredness is the gospel. The gospel reminds me of the amazing grace that's saved a wretch like me. The more we reflect on God's grace in our lives, the more our lives will reflect the character of Christ. Only then will we become parents who teach our sons and daughters how to lead like Jesus.

Who are the men or women in your life who've modeled servant leadership? Explain why you listed those people.

How are you currently modeling servant leadership to your family?

What one step can you take this week to start modeling servant leadership?

1. Paul David Tripp, "Happy Child=Easy Life," *Paul Tripp Ministries, Inc.* [online], 5 July 2013 [cited 22 May 2014]. Available from the Internet: *www.paultripp.com.*

GOD KNOWS YOU NEED HIS HELP

MATTHEW 11:28-29

PHILIPPIANS 4:19

It had been a long, hot day traversing one of the Florida theme parks. The day had gotten off to a late start, acquiring our tickets, which of course weren't where they were supposed to be. The skies opened up and a downpour of rain started just as we were waiting in line for a character picture. We pulled out our ponchos, hastily purchased from a drugstore that morning, and assumed we could outlast the storm.

We lasted all day, but we certainly didn't outlast the storm. Every inch of us was wet, but we only had one day to tour the park, so we pushed (or waded) through. It was hot and wet, and we were exhausted as we approached late afternoon.

As the eight kids in our party began falling apart one by one, I insisted we stop for a snack. We debated getting ice cream, but decided instead to visit a fruit stand. The sight of hot, tired, wet kids scarfing down fruit was delightful. We all, adults included, devoured the orange slices and over-priced grapes—so quickly in fact, we had to buy more before we left the stand. As a mom, I (Jen) knew we needed real nourishment.

Matthew 6:31-32 reminds us that God also knows exactly what we need. Matthew writes,

> *Therefore do not be anxious, saying, "What shall we*
> *eat?" or "What shall we drink?" or "What shall we wear?"*
> *For the Gentiles seek after all these things, and your*
> *heavenly Father knows that you need them all.*

Not only does God know exactly what we need to parent our children, but He's given us His Word to lead us. Let's devour it like orange slices and overpriced grapes after a tough day at a theme park.

→ START

How did it go this week, praying more intentionally for your children?

Have you ever done anything crazy because you were so tired from a lack of sleep? Share some of those experiences as a group.

Give examples of how God has given you true rest in your life.

→ WATCH

GOAL: To communicate that God cares more about our children than we do, therefore parents can find true rest.

VIDEO HIGHLIGHTS:

1. We're going to miss the mark as parents. The grace of God is sufficient for our shortcomings and failures.

2. We must place our hope not in our abilities as parents, but in the grace of God.

3. The gospel both shapes our hopes and sustains our dreams for our children.

Watch Session 7: *God Knows You Need His Help.*
Use the notes page to record key quotes and ideas that stand out to you.

NOTES

➤ DISCUSS

Most parents are thrilled when they learn they're expecting a child. However, it doesn't take long for the magnitude of what they're about to experience to sink in. All of a sudden they realize the responsibility. For many, the idea of bearing this responsibility becomes an oppressive weight around their necks rather than the blessing it's intended to be.

Parenting will only become a blessing when we realize that our identity isn't wrapped up in being a "good" parent or raising "successful" kids. Our identity is found in the truth that Jesus died in our place, and now through faith, not works, we have become children of God. If these are the lengths God would take to make us His children, then we can be confident that He will faithfully lead us as parents.

> *Come to me, all who labor and are heavy laden, and I will give you rest. Take my yoke upon you, and learn from me, for I am gentle and lowly in heart, and you will find rest for your souls.*
> **MATTHEW 11:28-29**

Are you tempted to build your identity on being a "good" parent or raising "successful" kids? If so, what does that struggle look like?

Parenting can be both challenging and difficult. What parenting challenges are you facing right now?

The apostle Paul beautifully reminds us in Romans 8:32, "He who did not spare his own Son but gave him up for us all, how will he not also with him graciously give us all things?" God is sovereign and keenly aware of every need we have as parents. Our responsibility is to trust faithfully in His design, parent as unto the Lord, and leave the rest up to Him. Remember, God knows we need His help!

Sometimes issues can move beyond challenges and become burdens. Are there burdens you're carrying related to your children that you need to release to Christ?

What are some of the means God has given to release your parenting burdens to Him?

What happens when you don't trust Jesus with your burdens? Can you think of a time where the strain of carrying burdens negatively affected your kids?

And my God will supply every need of yours according to his riches in glory in Christ Jesus.

PHILIPPIANS 4:19

As you reflect on your past, how have you seen the promise of this verse come to fruition? How does this give you confidence in raising your children?

As you look back on your time in this study, what's the one action step you're most convinced you need to implement (or have begun implementing)?

➤ WRAP-UP

1. Our identity isn't found in being a successful parent but in Christ.

2. Jesus calls us to lay our burdens upon Him and He will give us rest.

3. God will faithfully supply us with all we need to lead the next generation to trust in Him.

4. We must cease trying to control of our children and instead trust that God loves them far more than we do.

➤ PRAY

Spend the next few minutes praying with and for one another. Use the points below for guidance.

- Repent of the ways you have sought to build your identity on being a successful parent, and rejoice that your identity is found in Christ.

- Praise God for loving your children more than you do.

- Spend time sharing with God the burdens you are carrying regarding your children and let God give you His peace and rest.

Family Action Plan

After spending many weeks in a group studying together, you'll now be on your own navigating the waters of parenting. The great news is that "on your own" actually means "with God." You're never alone in your parenting journey because our children are God's first. They belong to Him and have graciously been entrusted to us.

God has given us means to accomplish the goals He has for us. This week, you'll go back through your study, noting steps you could take toward utilizing those means God has shown to you over the last few sessions. Also, feel free to use pages 110 and 111 for an easy reference to the Family Action Plan.

SESSION 1

Have you finished writing a family mission statement? If so, are you ready to edit it to reflect how you have grown in your understanding of parenting over the course of the study? Do that in the space below.

SESSION 2

What is your family's next Scripture memory goal?

SESSION 3

Check your calendar. Yes, again. Adjust it if needed.

SESSION 4

Are you beginning to fill your chart in as you listen to God regarding how to lead your family in His mission? Is there a phone call you can make or an event you can commit to that will jump-start making Acts 1:8 a reality for your family? Jot your thoughts down.

SESSION 5

Often, in the area of godly discipline, there are many older and wiser parents in our communities who can speak truth to us. Is there anyone you might want to share your chart with? If so, write those names down and seek those people out.

SESSION 6

How will you intentionally pray for the hearts of your children? Will you pray for them all each morning or one child a day? Make a plan for talking with God and listening to Him about your family.

➤ PERSONAL REFLECTION

"We love because he first loved us." 1 John 4:19

> *And Abraham lifted up his eyes and looked, and behold,*
> *behind him was a ram, caught in a thicket by his horns. And*
> *Abraham went and took the ram and offered it up as a burnt*
> *offering instead of his son. So Abraham called the name of*
> *that place, "The LORD will provide"; as it is said to this day,*
> *"On the mount of the LORD it shall be provided."*

GENESIS 22:13-14

I (Jen) cringe every time I read this story. I can't even begin to imagine sacrificing one of our children. In Genesis 22:2, Isaac is described as the one Abraham loves. What a significant description to remember as the story unfolds. As Abraham and Isaac traveled together to the land of Moriah, I wonder what they talked about. I imagine Abraham recounted Isaac's crazy birth story and shared with delight how God led Abraham and Sarah countless times. I wonder if they held hands or if Abraham hugged him tightly, reminding him God was faithful.

In what ways do you regularly show your children you love them?

As you read Genesis 22, you see in Abraham an unwavering trust in the Lord. The last thing he did before offering Isaac as a burnt offering was lead his son to worship the Lord. When he could have communicated fear, he showed faith. When he could have show despair, he chose trust.

How are you leading your children to worship the Lord?

Abraham's belief was counted as righteousness (see Gen. 15:6). We now have the blood sacrifice of Jesus as our righteousness. Romans 5:17 says that by Jesus, we will receive "the abundance of grace and the free gift of righteousness."

How do you feel knowing there's nothing you can do to earn righteousness?

We are only capable of loving our children because of what Christ has done for us. J.D. reminded us in the first session that loving our children is simply not enough. However, it does begin there. As 1 John 4:19 says, "We love because he first loved us."

God loves our children so much more than we do. They are His arrows, and He has entrusted us to launch them out into His mission. Are we ready?

➤ PERSONAL REFLECTION

What is Successful Parenting?

> *This Book of the Law shall not depart from your mouth,*
> *but you shall meditate on it day and night, so that you*
> *may be careful to do according to all that is written in it.*
> *For then you will make your way prosperous, and then*
> *you will have good success.*
>
> **JOSHUA 1:8**

People define success several ways. In our culture, success is often measured by things like the size of your bank account, your job title, the degrees you earned in school, your circle of friends, or the vacations you take. People spend their entire lives pursuing at all costs their vision of "success."

Parents also develop a vision of what successful parenting looks like. For example, some parents define success by having "well-rounded" kids. They push their children to thrive in school, participate in sports, play an instrument, and engage in community service. Others define success by having "morally upright" kids who are well-behaved and appear to have a good head on their shoulders. Even further, some parents define success by having kids who are "high-achievers," demanding excellence in academics, athletics, or some other realm.

There's nothing wrong with encouraging children to be well-rounded in their pursuits, morally upright, and excellent at what they do. However, none of these should become our vision of successful parenting. We must derive our vision for successful parenting from Scripture.

As God prepared Joshua to lead the people of Israel into the promised land, He reminded Joshua that his success as a leader was directly related to his obedience. God told Joshua to "be careful to do according to all that is written in it" (v. 8), meaning the Book of the Law. In other words, God was reminding Joshua to trust Him and His design, knowing that when he does, God will be faithful to accomplish His will.

We can't ultimately control what our children will do or become. All any parent can do is faithfully trust God and His design for parenting. By faith, we seek to fulfill our responsibilities and trust God to work in our children His glory. Proverbs 3:5-6 reminds us, "Trust in the LORD with all your heart, and do not lean on your own understanding. In all your ways acknowledge him, and he will make straight your paths." Success is found in our faithful obedience to God's design. We must remember that our identity is not found in successful parenting, but in Christ.

How have you defined successful parenting in the past? How would you define it now?

What steps of obedience do you need to take in order to follow God's design for parenting?

READY TO LAUNCH

FAMILY ACTION PLAN

Steps	Passage	Description
The Family Mission Statement, p. 18	Deuteronomy 6:4-9	A family mission statement helps your children remember the core values you've established as a family. To develop your statement, engage the whole family, identify goals based on Scripture, and work together. Find a creative way to display your mission statement in your home and continue to evaluate your progress periodically!
Teaching the Gospel, p. 32.	Psalm 119:9-11	One of our main responsibilities as parents is to teach our children the gospel. Help your children start memorizing Scripture—do it together as a family! Pick a verse, and make a plan for how you'll accomplish this goal. Explore different methods to help your children memorize their verse.
The Family Calendar, p. 48.	1 Timothy 3:5	Most of us have to be intentional about our schedules. Our schedules are full, but there always needs to be room to allow God to work in your family. Sit down with your kids and make a calendar of a typical week or month. Look at areas that affect your family time— what's non-negotiable? What can change? Are you leaving room for family time?

Steps	Passage	Description
The Acts 1:8 Strategy, p. 62.	Acts 1:8	This exercise is intended to lead you in developing an Acts 1:8 strategy for your family. We are God's mission strategy! Sit down with your kids and look at your local spheres of influence: schools, neighborhoods, teams, and community organizations. From there, look at places you feel uncomfortable. This could be inside or outside your city. Finally, discuss with your children different ways your family can share God around the world.
The Family Discipline Plan, p. 76.	Ezekiel 36:26-27	Share with your family that you'd like to establish some guidelines to help you be more consistent in your discipline. Create a chart that establishes consequences for the difficult behaviors you see in your children (refer to the chart on pg. 77). Discipline is difficult, but consistency will help. You'll be off to a great start at seeing the gospel transform your children's behaviors.
Praying Hands, p. 90.	Matthew 19:13-15	Trace your child's hand and use it as a prayer guide. In the thumb, write a goal you see God working on in them. In the pointer, write down your child's unique gifts. In the middle finger, name someone you'd like your child to emulate. In the ring finger, write a struggle your child has. In the pinky finger, write how your children are part of God's big story.

GROUP DIRECTORY

Write your name on this page. Pass your books around and have group members fill in their names and contact information.

Your Name: _____

Name: _____
Phone: _____
Email: _____
Social Network(s): _____

Name: _____
Phone: _____
Email: _____
Social Network(s): _____

Name: _____
Phone: _____
Email: _____
Social Network(s): _____

Name: _____
Phone: _____
Email: _____
Social Network(s): _____

Name: _____
Phone: _____
Email: _____
Social Network(s): _____

Name: _____
Phone: _____
Email: _____
Social Network(s): _____

Name: _____
Phone: _____
Email: _____
Social Network(s): _____

Name: _____
Phone: _____
Email: _____
Social Network(s): _____

Name: _____
Phone: _____
Email: _____
Social Network(s): _____

Name: _____
Phone: _____
Email: _____
Social Network(s): _____

Name: _____
Phone: _____
Email: _____
Social Network(s): _____

Name: _____
Phone: _____
Email: _____
Social Network(s): _____

Name: _____
Phone: _____
Email: _____
Social Network(s): _____

Name: _____
Phone: _____
Email: _____
Social Network(s): _____